PIANO · VOCAL · GUITAR

T0086616

SPIRIT CALLS

16 Inspiring Songs for Today

Uplifting Songs from Today's "New Thought" Songwriters and Artists

Featuring the Songs of:

Lis Addison

Jim Beloff & Herb Ohta

Karen Drucker

Lisa Ferraro

Michael Gott

Erika Luckett

Stefan Mitchell

Daniel Nahmod

Harold Payne

Faith Rivera

Charylu Roberts

Ruby

Bodhi Setchko

Teresa Tudury

Eddie Watkins, Jr.

Compiled by Charylu Roberts

Edited by Ronny S. Schiff

Library of Congress Cataloguing-in-Publication ISBN 978-1-4234-9524-6

Copyright © 2010 O.Ruby Productions · CD Compilation ℗ 2010 O.Ruby Productions

International Copyright Secured   Made in U.S.A.   All Rights Reserved

All Photos © 2010 Gary Jones   Used by Permission   All Rights Reserved

O.Ruby
O.RUBY PRODUCTIONS

EXCLUSIVELY DISTRIBUTED BY

HAL·LEONARD®

7777 W. BLUEMOUND RD. P.O. BOX 13819 MILWAUKEE, WI 53213

SPIRIT
CALLS
SERIES

ACKNOWLEDGEMENTS

All my thanks to Ronny Schiff, Lisa Ferraro, Bob Gordon, Karla Downey, Gary Jones, John Neff, Karen Drucker, Jim Beloff, Irwin Stein, Audrey Seymour, Bodhi Setchko, Matt Kramer, Rev. Karyl Huntley, Bryan Carroll, Bobby and Chuck Roberts, Robin Williams, Lori McMacken, Servet Hasan, Posi Lyon, Terri Beausejour, Sue Hayes, Lis Addison, and most of all to Jeff Schroedl, Keith Mardak, and all the folks at Hal Leonard Corporation.

- Edited by Ronny Schiff and Bobby Roberts
- Cover Design and Photography by Gary Jones
- Music Transcriptions and Arrangements by Bruce Cameron Munson and Chris Chandler
- Music Typesetting by Charylu Roberts and Bruce Cameron Munson
- CD Mastered by John Neff at Nightforest Studios

What is "New Thought"?

"New Thought" is a modern spiritual philosophy – based on ancient wisdom from both the East and the West – that stresses the unity of all life and asserts that a person's thoughts, beliefs, and attitudes determine his or her experiences in the world.

About the Spirit Calls Music Series

Spirit Calls is a series of New Thought music books and CDs designed to bring inspiration, peace, and harmony through the pure power of music.

Enjoy and be well!

CONTENTS

STAND TOGETHER

We were asked by Barbara Fields, the visionary executive director of AGNT (Association of Global New Thought), to create a song for its national convention. We wanted a soulful groove with lyrics that were positive, heartfelt, and uplifting—a song that could fit the event but also have a life beyond that purpose. Although we often share the stage, this was our first song collaboration. We were going for something that would be anthem-like without being cheesy—accessible, but with enough depth to bear repeat listening.

Words and Music by
Harold Payne and Faith Rivera

* All leads sung one octave below where noted.

1. Live the dream of your high-est call-ing.
2. Share your gifts with a world that's wait-ing

Be the hope of a new day dawn-ing.
for a change that we're all cre-at-ing.

We're the ones who can make a diff-'rence. Let's stand to-ge-ther.
It's the mo-ment for our great-ness,

let's stand to-geth-er now.___ Oh, oh.___ Mm,_ mm.___ Ah,_ yeah.

Ev-'ry-day's a chance you can do some-thing a-maz-ing to feel___

6

D.S. al Coda
(with repeats)

7

8

Bm

We're the ones who can make a diff-'rence, let's stand to-geth-er.
It's the mo-ment for our great-ness,

1., 3.
G

2.
G

let's stand to-geth-er now.

4.
G

Let's stand to-geth-er now.

D

(Lead vocals cont. ad-lib.)

Ev-'ry-bod-y, let's stand to-geth-er.

mf

Asus4

Ev-'ry-bod-y, let's stand to-geth-er.

Bm

Ev-'ry-bod-y, let's stand to-geth-er.

1., 2.
G

(with Lead vocals)

Let's stand to-geth-er.

3.
G

Let's stand to-geth-er now.___

D

Back-up only

Ev-'ry-bod-y let's stand to-geth-er.

EVERYBODY'S GOT A SMILE (FOR THE WORLD)

I wrote this song especially for the ABC television show, *Wife Swap*. I am the least likely person in the world to watch "reality" TV, which is what makes this so great! As a jazz singer, I had this steady club gig, and one afternoon the producers from *Wife Swap* called the owner of the venue to let him know that they were coming in on my night. They wanted to set up a scene where one of the swapped husbands goes out to a club and gets to sit in with the band. I performed all my original music, which aired on ABC's program, and wrote "Everybody's Got a Smile" as an easy blues tune the *Wife Swap* husband could sit in on and play to easily. Now I get to sing a happy blues tune that makes me laugh every time I do it. Keep on smiling! Life can be really funny.

Words and Music by
Lisa Ferraro

the world.___ You got - ta let it shine___ bright - ly,

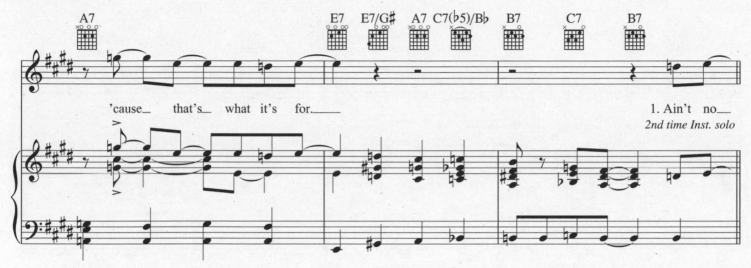

'cause___ that's___ what it's for.___ 1. Ain't no___

2nd time Inst. solo

___ sense in cry - in' when___ your life has___ got you___ down.___

Straight 8ths

A, a ___ ain't no sense in cry - in'___ when___ life has got

13

the world.___

You got - ta let it shine___ bright - ly

'cause___ that's___ what it's for.___

'cause___ that's___ what it's for.___

Yeah.

LEAN INTO ME

My inspiration as a songwriter comes from just paying attention to the moments of life as they unfold. Mundane or magic, I find material to work with everywhere, all the time. The poignancy of any message actually comes from the listener as he or she relates to the same things that I do. It's our mutual understanding and the strength of our connection and oneness that makes it powerful.

Words and Music by
Stefan Mitchell and Jonathan Kingham

Performance Note:
Verse 1 should be performed with a rhythmic underpinning of 6 against 4, which continues into the chorus. Verse 2 is straight 6.

1. When dark - ness clos - es in
2. long - ing to be filled with

and you can't find your way. The doubts you drag a - round
peace that ov - er - flows. To hear my qui - et voice

on - ly seem to say: how can you make it on your own? Re -
just be still and know in ev - 'ry sa - cred si - lence,__ I'm

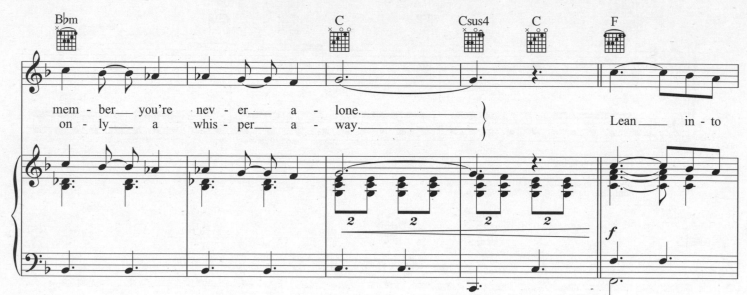

mem - ber__ you're nev - er__ a - lone.__
on - ly__ a whis - per__ a - way.__

Lean__ in - to

me,__ I will raise you up. Gath - er your faith__ and we'll

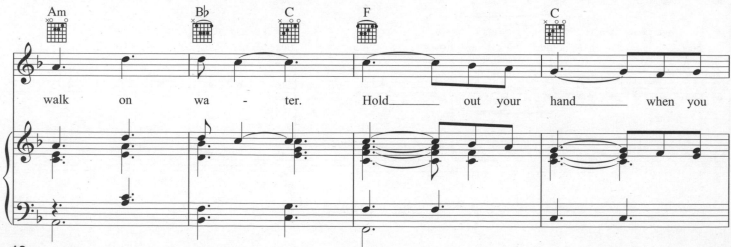

walk on wa - ter. Hold__ out your hand__ when you

me ___ I will raise you up. And gath - er your faith ___ and we'll walk on

wa - ter. Hold ___ out your hand ___ when you can't go on.

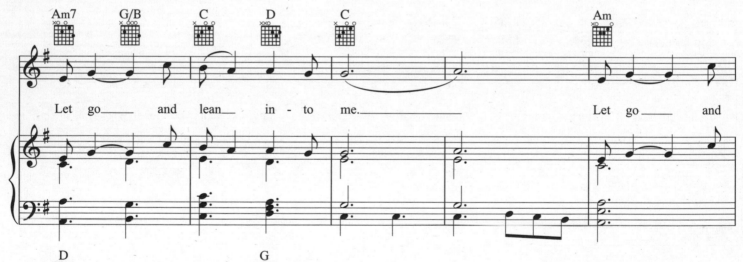

Let go ___ and lean ___ in - to me. ___ Let go ___ and

lean ___ in - to me.

LET IT SHINE

"**L**et It Shine" was a gift to myself when I turned fifty. This is an example of a song that took fifty years to brew and simmer inside of me, and about ten minutes to actually sit down and write. It's all about allowing myself to finally just let go of those mental chains and just shine. I truly believe we are all here to do just that—however it shows up—to just be the best that we can be and allow that light that is inside of us to shine.

Words and Music by
Karen Drucker

1. Gon-na' be the first on the dance floor, the first to raise my hand, the first to state my o-pin-ion, the first to take a stand. I won't play it safe and

wait for a sign. I'm gon-na' throw my-self out there__ and let my light shine. Let it

shine, let it shine.__ I'll let my big, bright, bril-liant beam of ra-di-ant light shine.

2. I'll be on "Op-rah" and "Co-nan," "Six-ty

Min-utes" and __ "The View." They'll all be talk-ing a-bout me, and all the things__ I do. I'll be the

one who sets_ the bar,_ the one who's in_ the know._ *Vogue* will come to me to see where

fash-ion trends_ will go._ 'Cause I shine, yes I shine,_ I'll let my

big, bright, bril-liant beam of ra-di-ant light shine. For too man-y years_ I

hid my light, fear-ing I was too much, and who I was just was-n't right. Then I

shine, yes I shine.___ I let my big, bright, bril-liant beam of ra-di-ant life shine.

Guitar solo

D.S. al Coda

For

Coda

give and re-ceive love." Give and re-ceive love." ___ 4. I am a

wom-an of pow-er, a wom-an of grace. The life that I've lived___ is in ev-'ry

23

THERE IS ONLY LOVE

This song is very special to me. I have sung it all around the world. I've had it sung back to me by audiences in Spanish and Russian. It reflects my deep conviction that we live in a friendly universe. Truly everything is for our good, if we're willing to look for the gift in each situation.

Words and Music by
Michael Gott
Second lyric by Karen Drucker

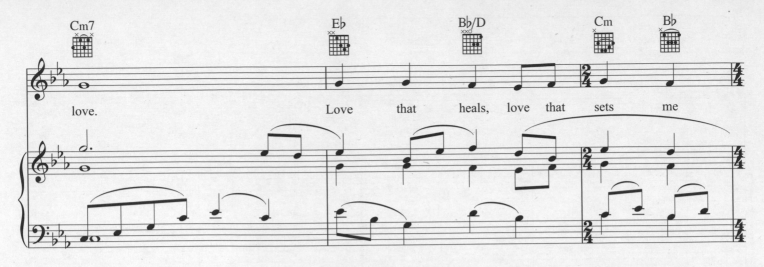

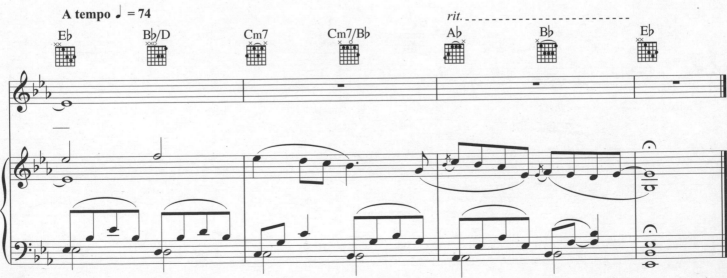

28

ALL IS WELL

The inspiration for "All Is Well" came out of a challenging time in the life of my wife and me. It was written as an affirmation to all of us to sing in the midst of confusion and uncertainty, a reminder not to allow our past mistakes to sabotage our "now." It's a declaration that right here and now, in this very moment, "all is well and unfolding as it should."

Music and Music by
Eddie Watkins Jr.

With spirit ♩ = 160

I'm not wor-ried 'bout to-mor-ow, to-day I de-clare:

"Free-dom from yes-ter-day,__ mis-takes of the past." To-day__ all things__

__ are made__ brand new,__ and don't it feel good__ to know__ that all is well__

and un-fold-ing as it should.___ I can change my re-al-i-ty___ by

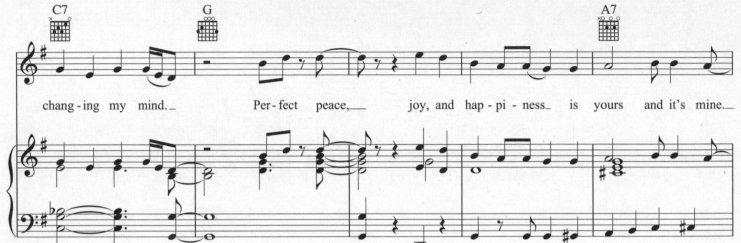

chang-ing my mind.___ Per-fect peace,___ joy, and hap-pi-ness___ is yours and it's mine.___

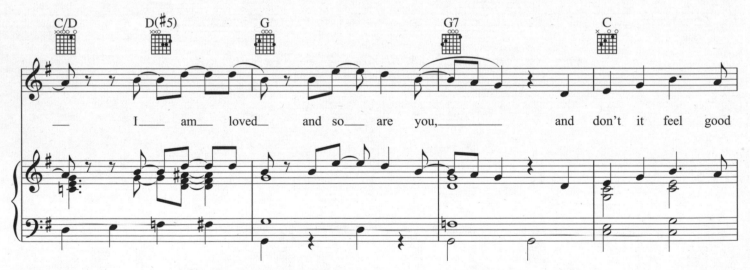

___ I am___ loved___ and so___ are you,_____ and don't it feel good

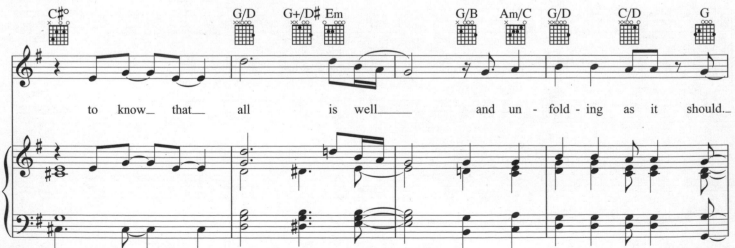

to know___ that___ all is well_____ and un-fold-ing as it should.___

Let me hear you say,__ "All is well,_____ all is well." Di-vine__

spir-it is di-rect-ing me right now.__ All is well,

all is well. All is well,___ and un-

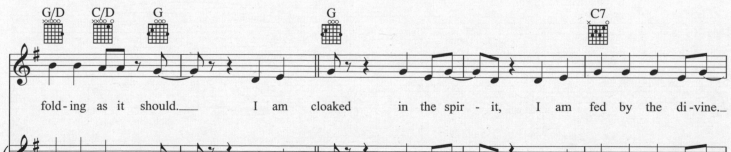

fold-ing as it should.__ I am cloaked in the spir-it, I am fed by the di-vine.__

*Lead Vocal ad-lib:

Don't it feel good just to know that my soul is free from time?
All I got to do is change my mind.

I'm free, ya'll. Don't it feel good?
All is well, and unfolding as it should.

Dust

My nephew inspired this song. As an adolescent struggling to make sense of the challenges facing him, he prompted me to write something that might ease his burden. Instead of feeling the insurmountable weight of fear and doubt, I wanted to show how each of us is a slice of a vast magnificence and that we have a choice in making our way through this grand adventure.

Words by
Erika Luckett and Amy Hurro

Music by
Erika Luckett

-tom giv-ing out.___ It's like giv-ing__ up, giv-ing__ up,___ pre-cious

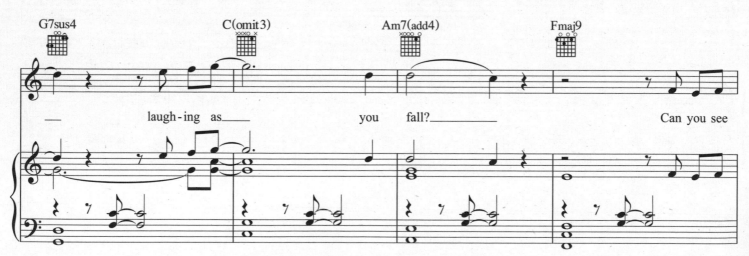

doubt. How___ does__ it feel skip-ping rope with your fears,_

_ laugh-ing as__ you fall?_____ Can you see

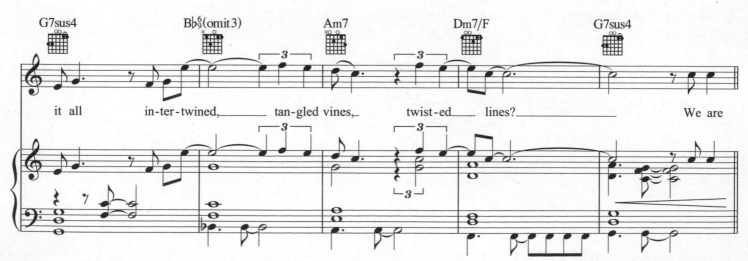

it all in-ter-twined,___ tan-gled vines,_ twist-ed__ lines?_____ We are

We are hand-fuls of dust, we are piec-es__ of sky. We are

thun - der-ing__ si - lence an - swer - ing why__ we're

gods in the ru - ins, god's__ in the mak - ing, we__ are... _____

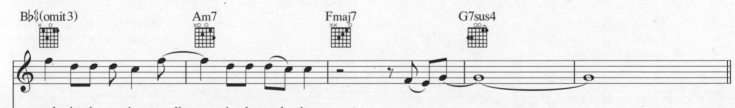

Peace Today

"Peace Today" was written on 9/11/06, a day I spent writing as many peace songs as I could. As a songwriter, it was the best thing I could do personally to honor the fifth anniversary of 9/11 and support the growing movement of peace and non-violence born out of such a tragic event. With each song, it became clear to me that the only lasting answer to violence and war is inner peace that is lived and practiced daily by each person on this planet. "Peace Today" is a pledge in song to choose peace at every turn and acknowledge the collective, transformative power of a committed community. I dedicate this song to the lone man who stood in the face of oncoming tanks on June 5th, 1989 at Tiananmen Square. His courage and peaceful power have never left my mind and heart since I saw his image on TV years ago.

Words and Music by Faith Rivera

lay down un-hap - pi - ness, and sur-ren - der to___ the peace___ I___ choose___
lay down self - right - eous - ness, and sur-ren - der to___ the peace___ I___ choose___

To Coda ⊕
(Verse 3)

to - day.
to - day.

My___ all___ I___ give, my___ love___

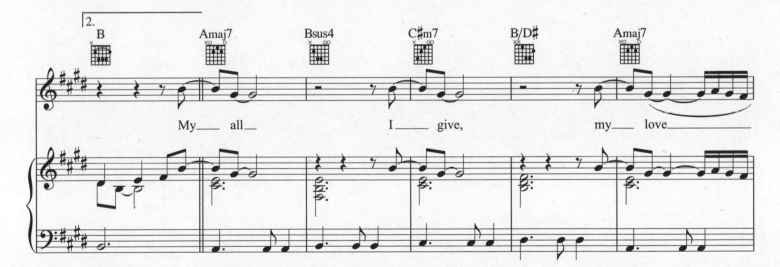

for___ all.___ My___ all___ I___

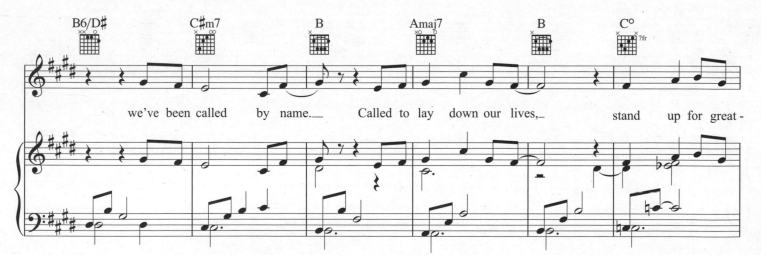

WITH A LITTLE BIT

Inever had the experience of waking up and writing a song in 30 minutes in a "spiritual" genre I'd never written in previously. I knew that—if not the song—the event itself was significant for me, and felt I had received a message of some kind. That message became clear a week later: When listening to a songwriter perform, I got the idea to do music books by celebrated performers of this specific genre, adding my own "inspired" song to the mix, and creating a compilation CD to go with each book. Patience, perseverance, and "a little bit" of faith have made this happen.

Words and Music by
Charylu Roberts

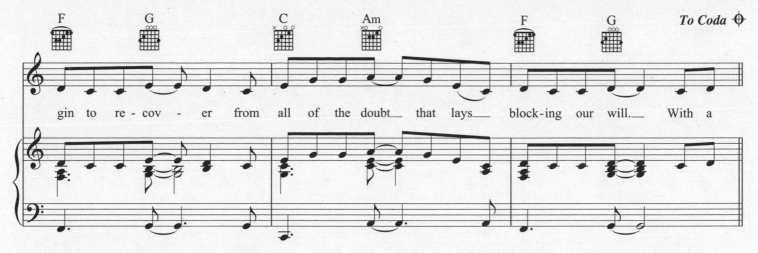

gin to re - cov - er from all of the doubt that lays blocking our will. With a

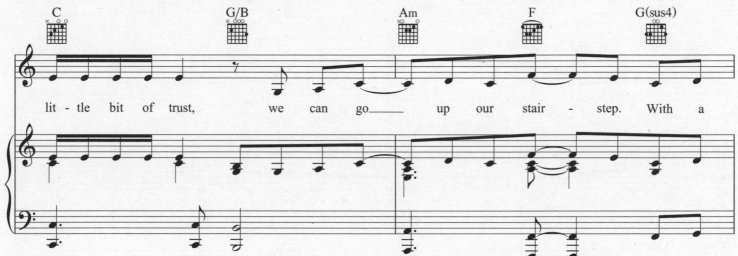

lit - tle bit of trust, we can go up our stair - step. With a

lit - tle bit of love, we learn to be - lieve in our - selves as a spir - it, be -

come our own lov - er, and spi - ral a - bove where

we can re - ceive. When we____ fall____ back____ to that dark place____ be - fore this, and

pull the cov - ers o - ver our spir - it, I

know, I know____ there is light just____ be - yond this,____

D.S. al Coda
(Opt. Instrumental solo)

light - er and bright - er than we've ev - er felt be - fore.

How Deep!

This song, "How Deep," arose when I was asked to be the soloist for a local church. The theme that week was "Spiritual Economics." With my strong connection to nature and family, it was not difficult to conclude that it is the simple things—the smell of the earth, the feel of the sun on my face, the sweetness of fruit from trees, the presence of my children when they enter a room, and my love for my husband—that make me feel wealthy. These things, which we take so for granted and which we cherish when they're gone, are what truly make us rich. This wealth grows deep in our lives and in the earth. All we need to do is recognize it and be thankful.

Words and Music by
Lis Addison

light,   a mo - ment that's com - plete (what more   do I   need?)

Moth - er Earth,   I   do walk   up - on you   with my feet.   With

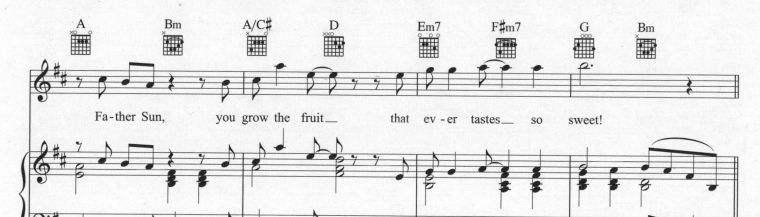

Fa - ther Sun,   you grow the fruit   that ev - er tastes   so sweet!

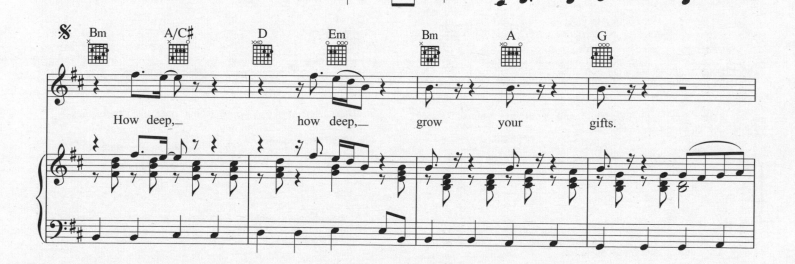

How deep,   how deep,   grow your   gifts.

47

How deep,__ how deep,__ grow your gifts.

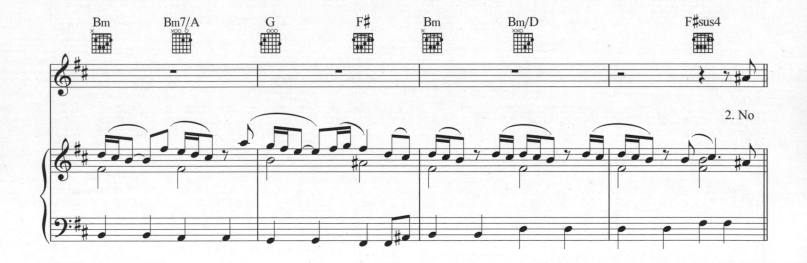

2. No

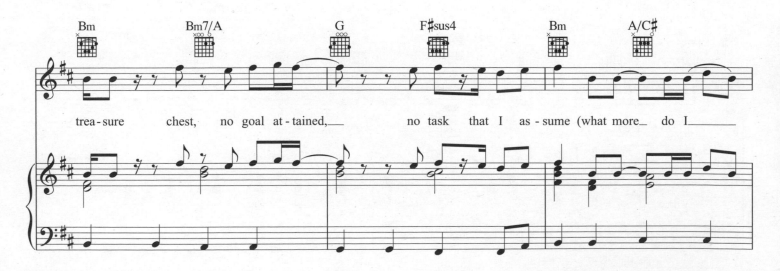

trea-sure chest, no goal at-tained,__ no task that I as-sume (what more__ do I__

need?) Makes me feel___ such joy as when you step in - to the room___

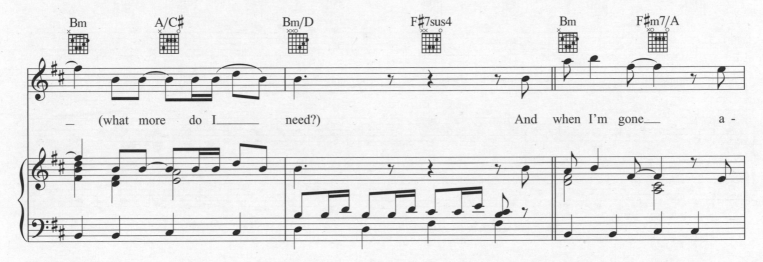

___ (what more do I_____ need?) And when I'm gone___ a -

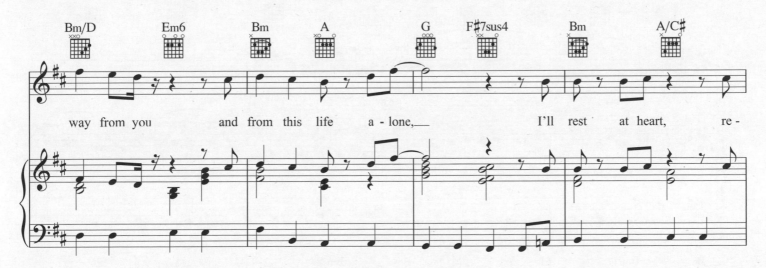

way from you and from this life a - lone,___ I'll rest at heart, re -

sid - ing in___ the love that we have known.

LIGHTEN UP

"Lighten Up" was created by me, for me, about me and a reminder for me to listen to everyday! I must admit I have a tendency to be a little hard on myself at times, and with all my songs, I write positive affirmations to help me remember the truth of who I am, and not what my inner critic would have me believe! This song—especially the chorus—helps me to remember that life is meant to be lived, enjoyed. I don't have to take it so seriously all the time! I can just have a good time and lighten up!

Words by
Karen Drucker

Music by
Karen Drucker and John Hoy

mat-ter an-y-way.__ Just en - joy your life. Get out__ of your way.__ "Light-en up!"

To Coda ⊕
(Bridge and Verse 3)

2. Now I'm head-

ed to a par-ty__ to meet my friends. I've got an out-fit that's to die for, hon-ey, I am

just the liv-ing end!__ But as I scope out the scene,__ it's ob - vi-ous to me__ that the mon-

ey at this par - ty, well it's simp - ly ob - scene.__ 'Cause they're talk -

ing a - bout their man - sions and their yachts, and drop - ping names, _ and in an in - stant I feel un - worth - y, small _

_ and a - shamed._ But as I try to make a bee - line, slip out the back door,_ I hear that voice_

_ say in - side of me say - ing once more,_____ "Light - en up."

D.S. al Coda

Do I stress?__ It's the thing__ I most feared.__ But then I re-mem-ber my new man-tra__ and I soon__ re-al-ize__ that I am per-fect, e-ven with wrin-kles and cell-u-lite__ thighs.__ I don't have to change a thing, strug-gle or try,__ 'cause my real__ beau-ty comes__ from__ deep__ in-side,_____ "Light-en up." Don't take it so

ser - i - ous - ly.___ "Light-en up." Trust the mys - ter - y.___ "Light-en up."

'Cause it does-n't mat-ter an-y-way. I'm gon-na en-joy___ my life and get out

of my own way.___ "Light-en up!" of my own way___ "Light-en up!" Don't take it so

ser - i - ous - ly.___ "Light-en up!" Trust the mys - ter - y.___ "Light-en up!"

On the Way of Love

How the song was written: Three artists. Hearts open. Rumi whispered. We listened.

Words and Music by Lisa Y. Ferraro,
Erika Luckett, and Kabir Helminski

live._____ So who's a - live?_____ The

one whose soul is born from love, whose soul__ is born__ from__ love._____

Guitar solo

Thun-der will rum-ble from out of the heart; from the bod-y, the soul__ will__ flash.

Light -'ning strikes___ from a tum - bl - ing cloud.___ The whole

D.S. al Coda

mead-ow greets the storm_____ of spring._____

Coda

Guitar solo

Gm7   Am7/G   Gm7   Am7/G   Gm7   Am7/G   Gm7   Am7/G

In love___ search for us.   In us___ search for this.   In love___ search for us.

CLOSER TO THE LIGHT

Herb Ohta's melodies are beautifully crafted. It can take weeks to write and polish a set of lyrics for Herb. This is important to know, because the writing of the lyrics to "Closer to the Light" was such a different experience. First of all, the melody (as usual provided on a cassette tape) was recorded as a mid- to up-tempo, happy little tune. After hearing it a few times, I was stumped. For some reason, I decided to slow the tape down on my cassette player. Suddenly, this happy little tune changed character and became more anthem-like. Then the magic happened: The title just came to me in an instant, and the lyric wrote itself in about 10 minutes. After writing furiously, I wasn't sure it was good or original. My wife, Liz, confirmed that it was indeed good, and that she couldn't think of another song like it. When other writers talk about songs that were dictated to them from somewhere out in the ether, I always think of "Closer to the Light."

Words by
Jim Beloff

Music by
Herb Ohta

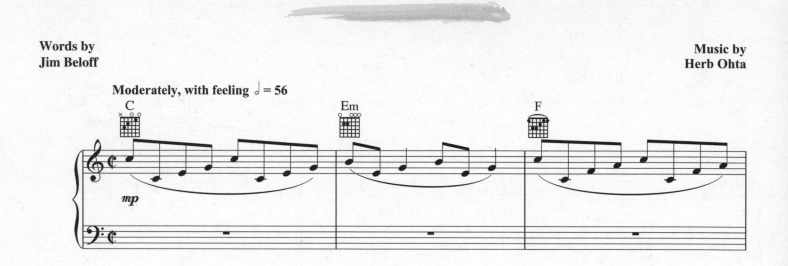

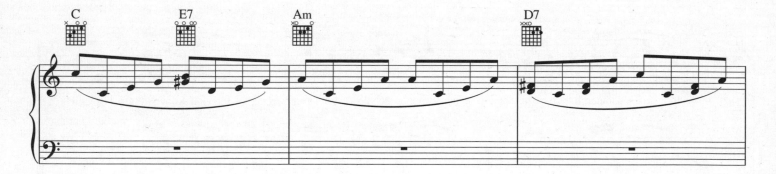

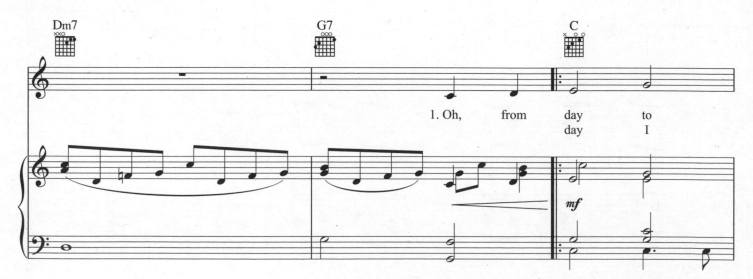

day,　　　it's so hard for me___ to say,___ if the
start　with this com - pass in___ my heart,___ and it

road that I'm___ on now___ will lead me right.___　　　Ah, but
helps to keep___ the road___ with - in my sight.___　　　And as

year　to　year,　　it be - comes a bit___ more clear,___　seems like
I　go　forth　looking for mag - ne - tic north,___　seems like

I am get - ting clos - er to___ the light._____ And when my
I am get - ting clos - er to___ the light._____ And when my

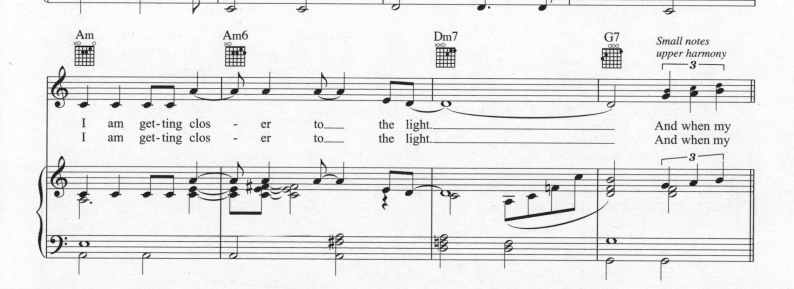

bur - den's great, so that I bend un - der the weight, and it____

seems like I'm sur - round - ed____ by_____ the night.____ Oh well, I____

don't mind trav - el - ing____ a - long this dark - ened road,____ if I'm____

trav - 'ling clos - er to____ the light._____ 2. Ev - 'ry

(unis.) *(unis.)* *Lead only*

To Coda ⊕

PEACE IS EVERY STEP

The inspiration for this song is quite simple. I had wanted to compose a new peace song for the end of each Sunday's service. One afternoon while reading the poetry book *Peace Is Every Step*, by Thich Nhat Hanh, I realized this simple affirmation could be remembered every day if there were a melody attached to it. It had to be simple, elegant and within an easy vocal range. I sat down at the piano and it flowed through me quite effortlessly in one sitting.

Words and Music by
Bodhi Setchko

ev - er - y____ breath, peace a - bides.____ I know the

joy of peace.____ I choose fear to re - lease.____

Ev - 'ry mo - ment love____ wakes up, and peace is ev - 'ry step.____

Peace is ev - 'ry step,____ peace is ev - 'ry step.____

If You Really Knew Who I Am

I had been in love with a man who didn't seem to recognize me at the time as his friend. A thought came to me that if he really knew who I was, he would love me. I wrote it as a sort of spiritual "pep talk" for my heart. In the writing of it, and then the performing, I was reminded of the sense of my own soul and its preciousness. Today, that man is still in my life and is one of my dearest friends.

Words and Music by
Teresa Tudury

And you'd know love_____ as you have nev - er known_ love,

* including vocal line: Csus/E

To Coda ⊕

And you'd be free._____ If you

real - ly knew_ who I am,___ you'd fill ev - ery room___ with

ros - es in bloom___ and_ shed glad_ tears.___ If you real-

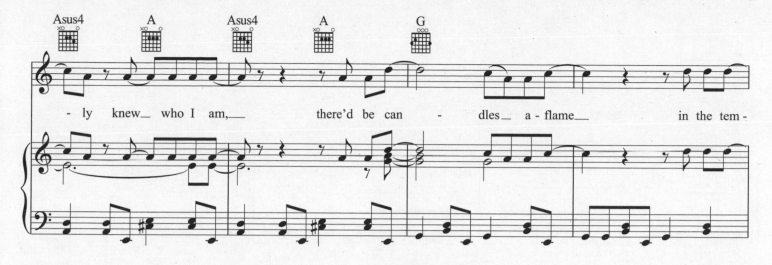

-ly knew___ who I am,___ there'd be can - dles___ a-flame___ in the tem-

D.S. al Coda

-ple to my name.___ And___ there___ we'd pray.___ And___ you'd know

Coda

real - ly knew___ how I am,___ you'd look deep___ in - to___ my

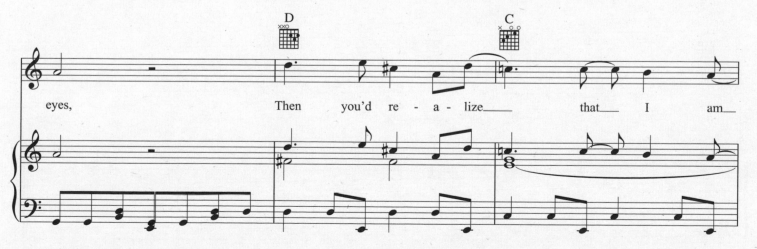

eyes, Then you'd re - a - lize___ that___ I am___

you._____ Then you'd re - a - lize___

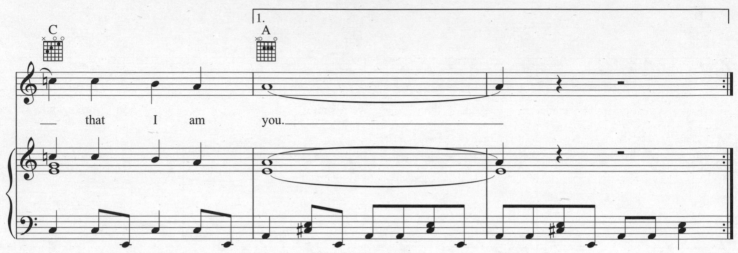

1.

___ that I am you._____

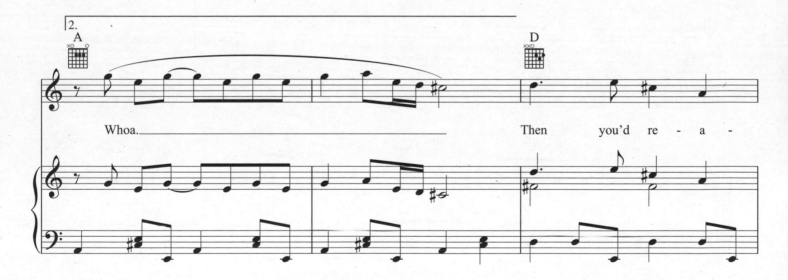

2.

Whoa._____ Then you'd re - a -

lize that I... If you real - ly knew___ who I am. ___

Last Song

"Last Song" was written under extraordinary circumstances in southeastern Utah, in a little town called Moab, in the heart of amazing red-rock scenery. On a hike one beautiful day, I spotted some cans and bottles left by thoughtless visitors, and resolved to clean up after them. I hauled hundreds of items into my car and down the road to a dumpster. It was one of the most joyful things I'd ever done. And I started thinking: This place is giving me so much joy, so much peace, so much inspiration. What if a one-mile stretch of "picked-up" River Road is all I can give back? In a larger sense, what can I hope to do with just my two hands, with just my few years on earth? What can any of us hope to contribute to such a big, complex world with such big, complex problems? Can I surrender my ego, and my desire to somehow change the world, or somehow live forever, and simply do the *good* that is right in front of me needing to be done? With that thought, I wrote "Last Song," which continues to be particularly resonant for me—an important reminder in my own life that there is always good to be done, if I simply open my eyes and my heart...and that uplifting one person, inspiring one child, picking up one bottle at the side of the road, is truly enough.

Words and Music by
Daniel Nahmod

when my bod-y's moved on, what will I have to show?_____ No, not

for - tune_ or fame;_ they scat - ter to the wind. The things that make a_ name_

___ just don't mat - ter in_ the end._ (shuffle) (But) is the world a lit - tle more peace -

- ful, o - ceans and sky_ a lit - tle more blue? Is hu - man - kind_ a lit - tle bit wis - er 'bout the good_

there's no-thing that I need to___ say. I have on-ly tried to serve;__ it's nev-er been a-bout

talk-ing an-y-way.__ So much hurt there is to heal; it's hard to un-der-stand.

All I___ can hope___ to feel__ is that I am do-ing what I can.   Is the

D.S. al Coda

(shuffle)

Coda

came.   Have I giv-en hope to the hope-less; has a hun-gry soul__ been fed?__

BIOGRAPHIES

Lis Addison is a composer, vocalist, and dancer, and writes music in her Singing Tree Studio for healing, dance, yoga, film and the concert stage. She has produced five CDs. Her latest one, *The Song of the Tree*, debuted at #2 on the NAR Charts and can be heard on national and international radio, "Guiding us to a higher vibration" (*Conscious Dancer Magazine*).

Ms. Addison holds a Masters degree in Composition and Electronic Music from Mills College as well as numerous certifications in dance, yoga and spiritual counseling. She has developed a sound and movement technique called KiVo®. Short for the Kinetic Voice, KiVo combines tribal dance and healing chants. She is an active instructor and performer. *www.lisaddison.com*

Jim Beloff is the author of *The Ukulele—A Visual History* (Backbeat Books) and author, arranger, and publisher of the popular *Jumpin' Jim's* series of ukulele songbooks. This series is sold worldwide and is distributed by the Hal Leonard Corporation.

Jim has also recorded two CDs of original songs performed on the ukulele, and in 2004, he released *The Finer Things*, a recording of sixteen songs he co-wrote with ukulele master, Herb Ohta.

In 1999, Jim and his family introduced a new, colorful, and low-cost ukulele called the Fluke and later a soprano-sized model, the Flea, that have won admirers all over the world. Jim and his wife Liz own Flea Market Music, Inc., a company dedicated to the ukulele. They regularly perform together worldwide, and believe very strongly in their company's motto, "Uke Can Change the World." *www.fleamarketmusic.com*.

Karen Drucker has recorded thirteen CDs of her original inspirational music and has won numerous awards for her songwriting, and for volunteer work in performing and producing shows for organizations in need. Her new book, *Let Go of the Shore: Songs and Stories that Set the Spirit Free*, was published by DeVorss Publishing this year. She has been a professional comedienne, led her own band for corporate events, and has been the music director for three different New Thought Churches, as well as music director and "music weaver" for many spiritual conferences and retreats.

Karen has been called "a master of communicating presence and spirituality through music." She loves making music, making a difference, and touching hearts. *www.karendrucker.com*

Lisa Ferraro is an inspired singer, songwriter, speaker, writer, and visionary. She is widely respected as a music director in the New Thought movement for her ability to tap into the energy of a room and connect soul-to-soul with her audience. In 2009, Lisa was asked to perform and co-direct the New Thought music team in Melbourne, Australia for the Parliament of the World's Religions. A talented songwriter who debuted some of her music with Marvin Hamlisch, she also has written songs for film and television.

She is currently performing as a solo artist and in collaboration with "Ruby," a trio with Erika Luckett and Kabir Helminski whose music is inspired by the poetry of 13th century mystic, Jalâluddîn Rumi. *www.lisaferraro.com*

Michael Gott is soloist and music minister at the Center for Spiritual Living in Reno, Nevada. He directs music and performs at many national and international conferences, including the United Centers for Spiritual Living's Annual Gathering, Asilomar, California and Circle of Love Gathering. He has released nine CDs. In addition to his musical abilities, Michael is also a speaker and teacher. He travels extensively across North America, and Europe singing and sharing his message of inspiration, transformation and Divine connection. *www.michaelgott.com*

Globally rooted, **Erika Luckett** carves her personal story from an international upbringing. Born in Mexico and raised in Venezuela, Brazil, and France, her world experience inspires the colorful and broad reach of her music. Erika has been honored as "One of the 100 Most Outstanding Women of the Year" by *Modern Women Today* magazine. Her music has earned awards including: Best Album of the Year, 2006, *Unexpected*, (JPF Music Awards), Best International Album 2006, *Unexpected* (*World Art Celebrities Journal*), and Best Independent Release of the Year, 2003, *My Little Crime, (Acoustic Guitar* magazine). She was the only musician invited to perform at the Nobel Peace Prize Forum. Her most recent collaboration, Ruby, with Lisa Ferraro and Sheik Kabir Helminski resulted in a performance at the 2009 Parliament of the World's Religions in Melbourne, Australia. *www.erikaluckett.com*

Stefan Mitchell is emerging as the vocal artist of awakening consciousness on the planet. His rich, multi-dimensional vocal style, poignant lyrical tapestries and captivating stage performance give listeners the soul-searing depth of a longed for spiritual connection. From the power that moves through his performances to his wry sense of humor, Stefan lives his belief that we are all made of one spirit. He feels that the deeper the recognition of that single spirit in our self and others, the sooner we wake up the world to a new and informed consciousness about our fate as individuals and that of the planet. *www.stefanmitchell.com*

Los Angeles-based recording artist and producer **Daniel Nahmod** has performed his powerful, heart-opening original music for over one million people since beginning his music career in 1999, selling over 75,000 CDs around the world and receiving literally thousands of standing ovations along the way.

Daniel's music has been heard on PBS and CNN, on commercial radio, in advertising, and on countless cable television programs. His songs and story have been featured in numerous magazines and books by the likes of Mark Victor Hansen (*Chicken Soup for the Soul*) and Robert Allen (*One-Minute Millionaire*). Fifteen of his songs have been recorded by over 50 artists in just the past five years.

A committed humanitarian, Daniel has presented his spectacular music for nearly all of the world's major faiths. He responded to Hurricane Katrina, 2004's humanitarian crisis in Asia, and in 2000, he was nominated as National Hospital Volunteer of the Year for his musical work at Cedars-Sinai Hospital in Los Angeles. *www.danielnahmod.com*

As a child growing up in Hawai'i, **Herb Ohta (Ohta-San)** was introduced to a wide variety of music including classical and modern jazz. This was of particular value when, at the age of twelve, Ohta met ukulele master, Eddie Kamae. In addition to teaching his young protégé a number of his techniques, Kamae encouraged Ohta to apply these approaches to the classical and jazz repertoire as well as the popular songs of the day. Ohta also studied music theory at the University of Hawai'i.

Since 1964, Herb Ohta has recorded seventy-plus albums/CDs and toured extensively throughout the world. He is especially popular in Japan. His 2008 CD, *Spotlight*, is a recording of songs with a Latin feel.

Harold Payne's songs have been recorded by such acts as Rod Stewart, Patti LaBelle, Kelly Rowland (of Destiny's Child) and long time collaborator, Bobby Womack—literally from Peter, Paul and Mary to Snoop Dogg. He created the Power of Positive Music™ series and is a Posi Music Award winner. Performing both solo and with his group Gravity 180, Payne is known for his uncanny ability to improvise songs. *www.haroldpayne.com*

Faith Rivera, Emmy-winning singer and songwriter, brings her musical message of peace to the world. With six solo albums, her transformational pop songs have been heard on TV and garnered numerous awards from New Age Album of the Year ("Suncatcher" JPF Music Awards) to Posi Music Awards ("Colors of Praise" and "Stand Together"). She's been featured with authors like Marianne Williamson to Jack Canfield, and has wowed audiences from the Hollywood Bowl to the Honolulu Symphony. Committed to peace and sustained abundance for all, she was named the 2008 Biggest Giver by Humanity Unites Brilliance, an organization providing food, water, education and micro-loans to women and children around the globe. *www.faithrivera.com*

Charylu Roberts conceived the idea for this book series after more than 30 years as a professional dancer, keyboardist, graphic artist, and music typesetter. She has helped to produce over 700 books for the print music industry. She is constantly moved by the way spirituality and inspiration can be conveyed through music. She has asked a handful of this genre's best musicians and songwriters to help a new generation of worldwide listeners find peace and feel uplifted through music. *www.orubyproductions.com*

Ruby, is the result of an inspired collaboration by three artists: vocalist, Lisa Ferraro; guitarist/vocalist, Erika Luckett and Kabir Helminski, translator of Rumi and Sufi poetry. Each had followed hers or his own creative path until a series of synchronicities brought them together in November 2007. Within fifteen minutes of their first meeting, a song came through inspired by the Rumi's poetry. It was as though the music had been waiting for these artists to come together. Their first collection of eleven songs inspired by Rumi's poetry was an effortless process, a receiving of treasures that had yet to take form. *www.WorldofRuby.com*

Bodhi Setchko is a multi-talented musician, songwriter, composer, recording artist, producer, teacher and professional band-leader. The founder of recording/touring ensembles, Crystal Wind and Rhythm Matrix, he has recorded 15 albums of original music. He has been the Music Director for the Golden Gate Center for Spiritual Living in Northern California since 2004.

His current project is Setchko and Meese, performing and recording with fellow musician, Stephen Meese. Having studied with many fine musicians, including renowned artists Paul Horn, William Mathieu, and G. S. Sachdev, he developed a unique style of improvisation using the sounds of nature as his inspirational source. His flute CD, *Trans Ukraine* was the #1 Ambient Album of the Year for 2006. *www.bodhisetchko.com* / *www.shamanicflute.com*

Teresa Tudury has been writing and performing from the age of 12. Music is not only her profession, but her life's path and she is grateful beyond words to know that.

Throughout her career, Teresa has recorded or performed with such greats as Leonard Cohen, Rickie Lee Jones, Lyle Lovett, Taj Mahal, Leo Kottke, Charlie Musselwhite, and Bonnie Bramlett. Now residing in Sonoma County, Teresa continues to perform and write new material. She has just released *Such Fine Things*, her latest CD. Her earlier recordings (1992 *Teresa Tudury*, and the 2002 *River Of Life*) were recently re-released. With these recordings and a steady stream of concert appearances, Teresa is a gifted artist in her prime. *www.teresatudury.net*

Eddie Watkins Jr. "My music is an expression of all the experiences of my life." Growing up in the ghettos of Detroit, playing bass on recordings with the Temptations and Marvin Gaye at 17, being "brought up" by the Motown Greats, becoming a studio musician, becoming wealthy, moving to L.A. with Motown, and substance abuse and recovering; all led to a spiritual search. When Eddie became involved in Religious Science in 1997, songs woke him up, and came pouring out of him. His first CD was selling within six months. His second CD, *We Come Together* was released in June of 2008. The third CD, *And So It Is* was released in June 2009. Eddie served three years as the Music Director at Center for Spiritual Living in Las Vegas and is currently the Music Director at Center for Spiritual Living in Seattle.

"I know that my life purpose is to share this music with the world." *www.eddiewatkinsjr.com*